The Story of
JOAN OF ARC

Gregory Guiteras

Text by Mary Carolyn Waldrep

DOVER PUBLICATIONS, INC.

Mineola, New York

Bibliographical Note

The Story of Joan of Arc is a new work, first published by Dover Publications, Inc., in 2002.

DOVER *Pictorial Archive* SERIES

This book belongs to the Dover Pictorial Archive Series. You may use the designs and illustrations for graphics and crafts applications, free and without special permission, provided that you include no more than four in the same publication or project. (For permission for additional use, please write to Permissions Department, Dover Publications, Inc., 31 East 2nd Street, Mineola, N.Y. 11501.)

However, republication or reproduction of any illustration by any other graphic service, whether it be in a book or in any other design resource, is strictly prohibited.

International Standard Book Number: 0-486-42385-9

Manufactured in the United States of America
Dover Publications, Inc., 31 East 2nd Street, Mineola, N.Y. 11501

INTRODUCTION

The year was 1429. France and England had been at war for nearly one hundred years, battling over England's claim to the French crown. In 1420, Charles VI of France, under pressure from his queen, Isabeau, and his uncle, Philip, Duke of Burgundy, signed the Treaty of Troyes. Under the terms of this treaty, Henry V of England would marry Charles' daughter, Catherine. Charles would continue to rule France, but after his death, Henry would rule both England and France. The treaty completely disinherited Charles VI's only surviving son, the future Charles VII.

Charles VI of France died in 1422; Henry V of England had died two months earlier. There were now two claimants for the throne—Henry's nine-month-old son and Charles VII, the teenaged Dauphin. France was split in two, with the English, joined by the Burgundians, controlling the north and the French controlling the south. The common people of France suffered greatly in the fighting.

In that year of 1429, an extraordinary figure appeared on the scene—one who would change the history of France. That figure was Joan of Arc.

FRANCE IN 1429

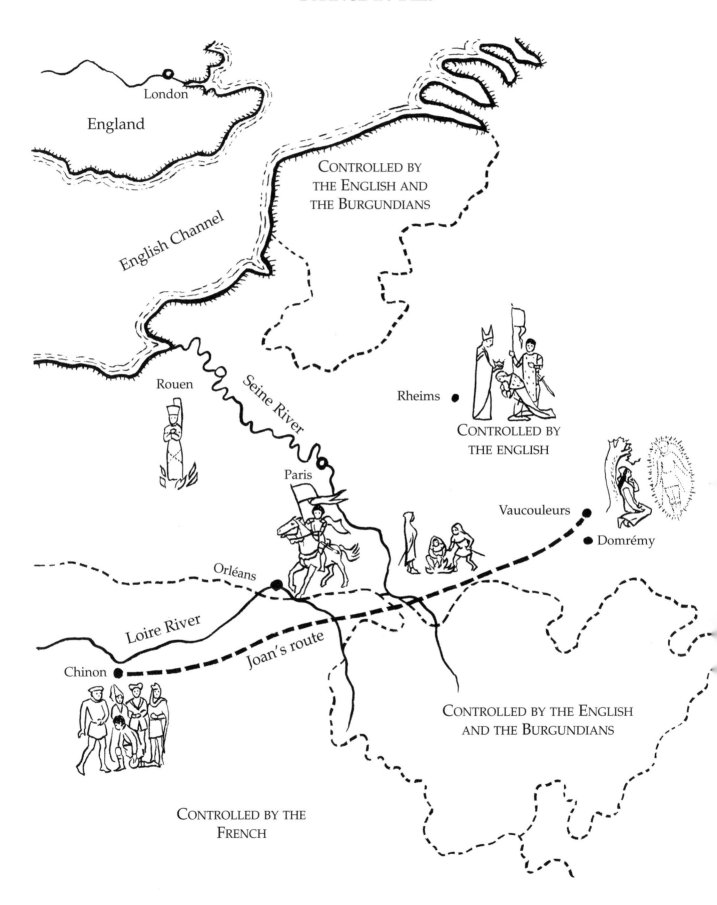

London

England

CONTROLLED BY
THE ENGLISH AND
THE BURGUNDIANS

English Channel

Rouen

Seine River

Rheims

CONTROLLED BY
THE ENGLISH

Paris

Vaucouleurs

Domrémy

Orléans

Loire River

Joan's route

Chinon

CONTROLLED BY THE ENGLISH
AND THE BURGUNDIANS

CONTROLLED BY THE
FRENCH

Joan of Arc was born in Domrémy, France, in 1412, the fourth of five children of Jacques and Isabelle d'Arc, relatively well-to-do peasant farmers. By all accounts, she was a normal child, if perhaps a bit more pious than her peers. Joan worked hard, both outside, in the garden or tending the family's livestock—a chore she hated—and inside, helping her mother with the spinning, weaving, and other household chores—work much more to her taste.

The little spare time Joan had was spent playing with the other children of the village. One favorite spot was a large beech tree at the edge of the nearby oak forest. This tree was known as the Fairies' Tree, for it was said that fairies had been seen there long ago. On certain special days, it was the custom to dance around this tree and hang garlands and wreaths on it. Joan joined her friends in these activities—a fact that would later be used against her at her trial.

2

Although Domrémy itself was loyal to the Dauphin, it was surrounded by Burgundian territory and the duchy of Lorraine. Throughout Joan's childhood, the village was at times raided by English or Burgundian troops, who burned the buildings and stole livestock.

When Joan was twelve, while working in her father's garden, she heard a voice telling her to be good and pious. A few days later, she heard the voice again, and again a few days after that. She realized that the voice was the Archangel Michael, leader of the armies of heaven. St. Michael told her that Saints Catherine and Margaret had been appointed to guide her. As Joan grew older, her voices began to tell her of the work that God had for her—to lead the Dauphin to Rheims to be crowned and to drive the English from French soil.

In 1428, Joan convinced a cousin to take her to Vaucouleurs, a fortress loyal to Charles VII, to ask Robert de Baudricourt, the captain of the fortress, to send her to the Dauphin to begin her task. Baudricourt laughed at her and sent her home, but she returned to entreat him again. According to legend France would be saved by a maid from an oak forest, and Joan's resolve and piety began to attract supporters who believed her to be this maid. Baudricourt eventually agreed to send Joan to the Dauphin at Chinon, 350 miles away, giving her a small armed escort.

In February 1429, Joan, now with shorn hair and dressed in men's clothing for practical reasons, and her escort began their journey on horseback. Part of the trip was through enemy territory, and the little group often traveled the back roads and at night to avoid English patrols. Eleven days after they began, Joan and her companions entered Chinon.

Shortly after her arrival, Joan was granted an audience with the Dauphin. The audience chamber was filled with over 300 richly dressed nobles. The Dauphin, an unprepossessing man who looked less royal than many of his nobles, was standing with a group of courtiers. Although no one pointed him out to Joan, she went straight to him and bowed, saying "God give you life, gentle king."

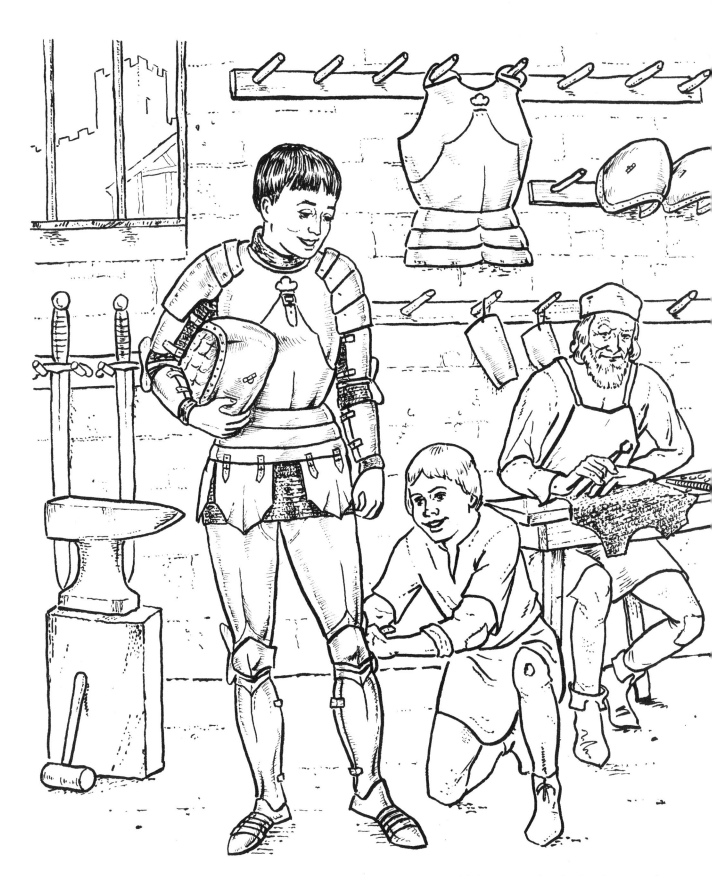

Joan convinced Charles that she was sent by God to aid him. Plans were made to assemble an army, and Joan was fitted for a suit of armor. She was offered a sword but refused, saying that her voices had told her of a sword that was buried behind the altar at the Church of St. Catherine in Fierbois. The sword, decorated with five crosses, was found exactly where Joan said it would be. Joan also had a banner showing Christ seated on a rainbow, with one hand raised in blessing and holding the world in the other. Two kneeling angels offered Christ the lilies of France. Joan's motto, "Jhesus-Maria," was written on the background in golden letters.

8

Joan's first task was to liberate the city of Orléans, then under siege by the English. She and her army entered the city on April 29. Joan was not in command of the French army, but was just one of its captains. Joan wanted to confront the English immediately, but the other commanders overruled her. The next day, she sent a letter to the English commander, urging him to lift the siege. Angered by his scornful response, Joan went out to the fortress of Les Tourelles on the bridge over the Loire River, where she demanded the English surrender. The English troops answered her with jeers and laughter.

9

Without Joan's knowledge, French troops attacked the fortress of St. Loup, just east of Orléans, in the hope that it could be taken before expected English reinforcements arrived. When Joan learned of the attack, she sped to the battle, which was not going well for the French. Her arrival rallied the French troops, however, and the fortress was taken.

Next, Joan convinced the other French commanders, who wanted to wait for reinforcements, that Les Tourelles could be conquered. On the morning of May 7, 1429, Joan led an attack against the southern outworks (a defensive position outside the fortress).

Joan had predicted that she would be wounded during the battle, and about midday, was struck in the shoulder by an arrow. She was carried to safety but returned to the battle after a short rest. By nightfall, the French were exhausted. After a break for food and rest,

Joan grabbed her standard, waving it with such vigor that the other commanders thought she was giving a signal. The French renewed the attack, storming the fortress and forcing the English to retreat.

During the retreat, the French set fire to the draw-bridge causing it to collapse. Meanwhile, the towns-people attacked Les Tourelles from the rear. The English abandoned the city and Orléans was liberated. The next morning, Sunday, May 8th, Joan and the other commanders reentered the city to great rejoicing.

Ten days after she arrived in Orléans, Joan left to join the Dauphin in Tours. Once there she convinced him to go to Rheims, where the kings of France were traditionally crowned. Rheims was in the English-held region of Champagne, and Joan and the army had to fight their way to the city. After a series of remarkable victories, Joan and the Dauphin entered the city. On July 17, 1429, Charles VII was crowned in the Cathedral of Rheims.

Following the liberation of Orléans and the coronation of Charles VII, Joan's fame spread far and wide and her popularity soared. Wherever she went the people, especially the children, wanted to see her and touch her and to offer her their thanks.

15

Joan and the army, under the command of the Duke of Alençon, were eager to press the attack and drive the English out of France. Charles, however, hesitated, agreeing to a truce. Joan and Alençon, impatient with the delay, led an unauthorized attack on Paris, with lit-

tle success. During the battle, Joan was once again struck by an arrow, this time in the thigh. The king ordered the French to return to Saint-Denis, where he was in residence.

Sick at heart over the defeat at Paris, Joan went to the Cathedral of Saint-Denis. There, she made an offering to the Virgin Mary—the armor she had worn at Paris, together with a sword captured during the battle.

Some months later, Joan took a small force north to harry the English and Burgundian forces; however, Joan's voices told her that she would soon be captured. On May 23, 1430, the French attacked the Burgundian forces near the town of Compiègne. When English and Burgundian reinforcements arrived, the French began to retreat back into the city. Joan suddenly found herself isolated from her men. During the fighting, a Burgundian archer pulled her from her horse. She was now a captive.

18

Joan was a great prize and several factions wanted her. She was first turned over to Jean de Luxembourg, a Burgundian. In November, in return for 6,000 francs, Luxembourg delivered her to the English, who eventually took her to Rouen. There she was imprisoned in a narrow, damp cell and chained hand and foot, guarded by brutal English men-at-arms who heaped abuse on her and kept her in fear of being assaulted.

Although Joan was held by the English it was the Inquisition who was to try her on charges of heresy. Joan begged to be transferred to a Church prison, but the English were taking no chances with their important prisoner. The charges against her included the fact that she dressed in men's clothing, "an abomination to God" according to the Church, and that she claimed to be guided directly by God through her voices. The Church, as God's representative on earth, believed itself the only agency that could convey God's intentions to the

20

people. Joan's trial, which began in January 1431, was run by Pierre Cauchon, Bishop of Beauvais, who was eager to convict her. He selected more than fifty churchmen to serve as judges for the trial. The court held its first public session on February 21. Joan, pale and drawn from her imprisonment, still wore men's clothing, a fact that shocked many of the clergy and monks present.

For four months, Joan was examined relentlessly by the judges. The uneducated peasant girl, however, held her own against the learned churchmen. When asked if she knew whether she was in God's grace—something no Christian could claim to know—she replied, "If I am not in God's grace, I pray God to put me there; if I am, may God keep me there." Toward the end of May, Cauchon declared the trial to be over. He pronounced her a heretic to be turned over to English justice. Joan, frightened and feeling abandoned by her voices, panicked, signing a document in which she agreed to wear women's clothing and obey the Church in all things. She was sentenced to life imprisonment.

As a penitent, Joan expected to be removed to a Church prison, guarded by nuns and priests, but Cauchon had her returned to her cell and put back in chains. Saint Catherine and Saint Margaret appeared to her in a vision, expressing God's sorrow that she had renounced her voices. Although she was now dressed in women's clothing, her male clothing had not been taken from her. Soon, she once again was dressed as a man.

Early on May 30, 1431, Joan was told she was to be burned at the stake within the hour. She was dressed in women's clothing and on her head was placed a paper cap with the words, "heretic, relapsed, apostate, idolatress" written on it. Under heavy guard, she was brought to the Old Market Square where a large crowd of clergy, soldiers and common people had gathered to see her execution. She was placed on a platform across

24

from a large dais where her judges sat. After she was forced to hear a lengthy sermon, Bishop Cauchon once again pronounced her cast out of the Catholic Church and turned her over to the state for justice. Joan began to weep and pray aloud, begging mercy from God and forgiving those who had wronged her.

When Joan asked for a crucifix, an English soldier hastily tied
two pieces of wood together to form a cross and gave it to her.

The executioner lit the pyre. A sympathetic priest brought out a crucifix from a nearby church, holding it high so that Joan could see it. From the flames Joan called upon the name of Jesus several times, as she died a martyr, moving many in the crowd, including some soldiers, to tears. One witness claimed to see the word "Jesus" in the flames; another thought he saw a dove rising from the pyre.

Joan's story did not end with her death. Twenty-six years after her execution, a new trial was convened and the first trial nullified. In 1920, the Catholic Church named her to the catalogue of saints, and the simple peasant girl who did so much to save France became its patron saint. Her life has been celebrated in art, drama, and literature. She has inspired numerous paintings, statues, books, plays, and movies. Even today her story is still being told.